Belief in the Creator is the surest foundation of any civilization. Selassie I

HELP SPREAD THE WORD BY SUPPORTING THE COST OF THIS BOOK, OR MAKING LEAFLETS.

"It is one of the tragedies of Our day that half of the world's population is wracked by a never satisfied hunger and remains poverty-stricken, disease-ridden and ignorant, vast amounts are spent by great powers on armaments, money which, if diverted to satisfying the basic human needs of the poorer people of the world, could transform their lives and restore to them their human dignity, their happiness in the present and their confidence and faith in the future." - His Imperial Majesty, Emperor Haile Selassie I

… It is not enough for the children of Ethiopia to be recipients of education. They should never forget that the responsibility for passing on this knowledge to others and of handing it over to the next generation rests on them. …"

There is no one *anywhere in the world who does not cherish the hope of having his standard of living* raised. Selassie I

You can find a lot of information about human rights but it is not always easy to understand. It can be hard to see how human rights can be part of your life. This booklet tells you about some human rights and how they can help you.

We are making a lot of our information into easy read so that everyone can understand more about human rights and the law.

What is the Equality and Human Rights Commission?

The Equality and Human Rights Commission works to make sure that people are treated fairly and equally

We are working to stop discrimination against disabled people, men and women and people from different races and cultures.

Discrimination
means treating someone worse than other people for some reason

We also want to make sure that people's human rights are respected.

Human rights
are basic rights and freedoms that belong to every person in the world.

The Human Rights Act is the law about human rights. Many other laws have to follow what the Human Rights Act says.

Human rights are about how we treat each
other. They are about

- respect
- freedom
- equality
- dignity
- fairness.

The Human Rights Act protects everyone.

The right to life
– this means that your life is as important as anyone else's.

The right to dignity and being part of the community
– this means that you should get the care and support you need to have a good life.
You should also be able to join in with things in your community along with everyone else.

Article 9 Freedom of religion

The right to freedom of thought, conscience and religion includes:

- the freedom to change religion or belief;
- the freedom to exercise religion or belief publicly or privately, alone or with others;
- the freedom to exercise religion or belief in worship, teaching, practice and observance;

Freedom of religion does not prevent there being a state church, but no one can be forced to join a church, be involved in its activities or pay taxes to a church.

The role of the State is to encourage tolerance and all religions or non-religions, if regulated, must be regulated with complete neutrality.

The right to exercise, or manifest, one's religion or belief will not generally be considered to be interfered with if a person is left with a choice as to whether or not to comply with his or her religious obligations. However, there will be interference if restrictions make it practically difficult or almost impossible to exercise the religion or belief.

Example of a Human Rights Case

R (Williamson and others) v Secretary of State for Education and Employment and others (2005)

Article 9 was invoked in an attempt to overturn the ban on corporal punishment of children by teachers. It was claimed that part of the duty of education in the Christian context was that teachers should be able to stand in the place of parents and administer physical punishment to children who were guilty of indiscipline. The House of Lords found that the statutory ban pursued a legitimate aim and was proportionate. Children were vulnerable and the aim of the legislation was to protect them and promote their wellbeing. Corporal punishment involved deliberately inflicting physical violence. The legislation was intended to protect children against the distress, pain and other harmful effects this infliction of physical violence might cause.

Human rights are for everyone.
They are to help groups like councils, the police and hospitals protect you by making sure they respect your human rights

Human rights mean that the government should protect all of us from groups or individuals who would take away our rights.

MANY PEOPLE JUST THINK THE POLICE OR GOVERNMENTAL PEOPLE SHOULD KNOW AND ABIDE BY THEE LAWS, BUT THIS IS NOT THE CASE IN MUCH CASES, AND IN THE END A MAN IS JUST A MAN HE CAN BE CROOKED WITH NO COMMANDMENTS AND RELIGION BEHIND HIM.

Until The
Philosophy
Which Holds
One Race
Superior And
Another
Inferior
Is Finally
And Permanently
Discredited
And Abandoned.....
Until That Day
Everywhere Is War...

Haile Selassie I

"I must say that, black and white as forms of speech, as means of judging mankind, should be eliminated from human society.

Human beings are precisely the same, whatever colour, race, creed or national origin they may be."

Haile Selassie I

The human right to health means that everyone has the right to the highest attainable standard of physical and **mental health**, which includes access to all medical services, sanitation, adequate food, decent housing, healthy working conditions, and a clean environment.

THE TERM HEALTH DIFFERS DEPENDING UPON EACH INDIVIDUAL

SOME FEEL THEY MUST SWIMM IN THEE RIVER OR OCEAN EACH DAY

OTHERS FEEL THEY MUST LIFT DANGEROUS WEIGHTS.

SOME FEEL THEY MUST MAKE LOVE EACH DAY

OTHERS FEEL THEY MUST WAIT AND DENY LOVE.

Protection from slavery and forced labour

The Human Rights Act protects your human right not to be held in slavery or servitude.

Slavery is when someone actually owns you like a piece of property.

WHEN YOUR WHOLE SOURCE OF BEING YOUR FOOD AND SHELTER IS DEPENDANT UPON A WAGE OR A BENEFIT THAT IS NOT GUARANTEED.

HUMAN RIGHTS ACTS ARE GENERALLY BASED UPON ONES COMMANDMENTS AND RELIGIOUS BE-LEAFS AND PRINCIPLES, AS MUCH OF THE COMMUNITIE ACTIVITIES AND WORKS MAY OFFEND ONE'S RELIGIOUS BELEAFS,

EACH AND EVERY CONFRONTATION MUST BE PEACEFULLY RESOLVED BETWEEN MEMBERS OF THEE COMMUNITIE AND GOVERNMENT

THE RIGHT TO BE FREE

Many times in his writings, particularly in The Synthesis of Yoga, Sri Aurobindo warns us against the imaginings of those who believe they can do sadhana without rigourous self-control and who heed all sorts of inspirations, which lead them to a dangerous imbalance where all their repressed, hidden, secret desires come out into the open under the pretence of liberation from ordinary conventions and ordinary reason.

One can be free only by soaring to the heights, high above human passions. Only when one has achieved a higher, selfless freedom and done away with all desires and impulses does one have the right to be free.

But neither should people who are very reasonable, very moral according to ordinary social laws, think themselves wise, for their wisdom is an illusion and holds profound truth.

One who would break the law must be above the law. One who would ignore conventions must be above conventions. One who would despise all rules must be above all rules. And the motive of this liberation should never be a personal, egoistic one: the desire to satisfy an ambition, aggrandise one's personality, through a feeling of superiority, out of contempt for others, to set oneself above the herd and regard it with condescension. Be on your guard when you feel yourself superior and look down on others ironically, as if to say, "I'm no longer made of such stuff." That's when you go off the track and are in danger of falling into an abyss.

(The Sunlit Path. Words of The Divine mother)

Development

Although the beginnings of civilization of each country vary in time, the fundamental factors which gave impetus to each country to awaken and embark on the road to progress to reach their present level of development, are those qualities which are enshrined in the nature of man, namely desire and fortitude.

The partner who places his own short-range ambitions ahead of the long-range interests of the partnership has embarked on a course which will ultimately result in the dissolution of the partnership itself.

It is by the understanding of past difficulties that we can bequeath fundamental guidance which would be of pride to the coming generations we therefore urge our people to struggle and to make sacrifices for those things which will enable them to ameliorate their conditions of life and leave a richer heritage. **Selassie I**

Social Development

Lasting progress can only be built on deep and enduring foundations. When a solid foundation is laid, if the mason is able and his materials good, a strong house can be built.

To develop oneself, one has to develop one's own initiative and perseverance - a man has to strive in order to grow. Let us work out our own programmes in all fields - political, economic, social and military. Man's contributions which live to influence the life and progress of posterity, are the most permanent monuments that can ever be created. We must become increasingly willing to analyze our efforts, to experiment, to admit our failures as we take pride in our successes. **Selassie I**

Me personally I beleave in Selassie I's Holy commandments, and Do not agree with the ideology of freewill to behave as we wish, and without Grace for all things down to thee breath of life and drink of water I feel we deserve nothing much as a nation. Wake up from your Dreams my people, Think about if you was the primminister, government, mp etc Is this thee world you wood create? Do you agree with the system?, Wood everybody have to work to eat? Wood you authorise money to control us? So why are wee as a nation allowing one man to decide for us how we should live, is he GOD (JAH). Is his word more powerful than that of the Holy Bible's Instruction unto mankind?

KNOW YOUR HUMAN RIGHTS

ONE HAS THEE RIGHT TO REJECT ALL UN-GODLY LITERATURE

ONE GOD FOR US ALL UNITED NATIONS

Although many find fault in there government, wee should take time to relise each and every government is directed by its people. And thee system is a refletion of human behaviour, ie if thee communitie had 100 people residing in it, and a 100 people were vegetarians, then there wood be no non –vegetarian food in thee communitie. If a 100 people voted God (Jah) was our leader, then no man wood be able to have leadership.

Psalm 68:4

Sing unto God, sing praises to his name: extol him that rideth upon the heavens by his name **JAH**, and rejoice before him.

Each and Every Individual has thee Right to Live in peace and Harmony, within their community, Human Rights are laws governed to protect our individual Liberty's, that wee may face in raspect untoo Our be-leafs, our principles and our Dignity, and most importantly Our general view upon what is Right and Wrong. Most cases are generally against thee government and a Individuals or Churches beleaf.

WORK AND FORCED LABOUR (Protection from slavery and forced labour)

The term forced labour is significant unto every individual upon thee earth, as no child should be made to feel they have to do anything more than give Grace to eat and be sheltered. But History shows many people have been forced to sign Job seekers agreements, and threatened there benifits will stop if they do not, taking away there source of life to feed.

It could be said thee only reason this is possible to happen is there neglection of Spiritual Education ie. The Holy Bible, as it wood be obvious to some they were not here to work for monie or beg for benefits.

Ecclesiastes 8:15
Then I commended mirth, because a man hath no better thing under the sun, than to eat, and to drink, and to be **merry**: for that shall abide with him of his labour the days of his life, which God giveth him under the sun.

For those whom Did not know, If One does not agree with money as being a part of Life, And Do not agree one must have to work for a living, and will accept no form of paid works, One has thee Right to be Offered Charity works or Volutary works, or Non-tax organisations rolls.

Voluntary organisations rely on people who would rather do something useful for next to nothing than something destructive for many times more. Most Governments offer some sort of voluntary works

Basically all charity works and non tax voluntarily works is a symbol of love and devotion unto ones community development and Spiritual awareness, and paid works are a symbol of greed and a Individuals desire to please Oneself and his household, a community breakdown ,as people wood not have time to be community members, and our leisure time wood be minimal.

Where does freedom from forced labour originate from?.

.. EXODUS CHAPTER 5 NEW JERUSALEM BIBLE

1 After this, Moses and Aaron went to Pharaoh and said to him, 'This is what Yahweh, God of Israel, says, "Let my people go, so that they can hold a feast in my honour in the desert." ' 2 'Who is Yahweh,' Pharaoh replied, 'for me to obey what he says and let Israel go? I know nothing of Yahweh, and I will not let Israel go.' 3 'The God of the Hebrews has encountered us,' they replied. 'Give us leave to make a three -days' journey into the desert and sacrifice to Yahweh our God, or he will strike us with a plague or with the sword.' 4 The king of Egypt said to them, 'Moses and Aaron, what do you mean by distracting the people from their work? Get back to your forced labour.' 5 And Pharaoh said, 'Now

that the people have grown to such numbers in the country, what do you mean by interrupting their forced labour?' 6 That very day, Pharaoh gave the order to the people's taskmasters and their scribes, 7 'Do not go on providing the people with straw for brickmaking as before; let them go and gather straw for themselves. 8 But you will exact the same quantity of bricks from them as before, not reducing it at all, since they are lazy, and that is why their cry is, "Let us go and sacrifice to our God." 9 Give these people more work to do, and see they do it instead of listening to lying speeches.' 10 The people's taskmasters and scribes went out to speak to the people and said, 'Pharaoh says this, "I shall not provide you with any more straw. 11 Go and collect straw for yourselves where you can find it. But your output is not to be any less." ' 12 So the people scattered all over Egypt to gather stubble for their straw. 13 The taskmasters harassed them. 'You must complete your daily quota,' they said, 'just as when the straw was there.' 14 And the Israelites' foremen whom Pharaoh's taskmasters had put in charge of them, were flogged and asked, 'Why have you not fulfilled your quota of bricks made today as before?' 15 The Israelites' foremen went and appealed to Pharaoh. 'Why do you treat your servants like this?' they said. 16 'No straw is provided for your servants, yet still the cry is, "Make bricks!" And now your servants are being flogged!. . .' 17 'You are lazy, lazy,' he retorted. 'That is why you say, "Let us go and sacrifice to Yahweh." 18 Get back to your work at once. You will not be provided with straw; all the same, you will deliver the quota of bricks.' 19 The Israelites' foremen saw they were in a difficult position on being told, 'You will not reduce your daily production of bricks.' 20 As they left Pharaoh's presence, they met Moses and Aaron who were standing in their way. 21 'May Yahweh look down at you and judge!' they said to them. 'You have brought us into bad odour with Pharaoh and his officials; you have put a sword into their hand to kill us.' 22 Moses went back to Yahweh and said, 'Lord, why do you treat this people so harshly? Why did you send me?23 Ever since I came to Pharaoh and spoke to him in your name, he has ill-treated this people, and you have done nothing at all about rescuing your people.'

This story is before Jah's holy commandments unto his people, If our purpose in life is not for thee protection of humanity , ie thee trees , rivers her earth, then humanity will punish us and take thee straw from our hands and pasture from our feet and give us bricks to destroy ourselves and build 4 wall cells to enjoy the concrete life the city life of greed and vanity.

One has thee Right to a Benefit that is appropriate unto ones needs, Ie, whether one has dependent children, whether One Travels, Night Life, etc. One has thee right to a benefit of thee working class, or one has thee right to live within a community environment

No Individual Shall be Denied benefits or forced to sign documentation in seeking work, after stating one will accept Charitable works or voluntary. As accepting charity or voluntary works one shall be offering to be of service unto their communities development and well being.

One Has thee Right to Disagree with any work whatsoever, And is not obliged to sign Documentation in seeking work, As many may feel threatened if they Do not sign on at thee Job Centre's they may lose their benefits,

This Act is a Violation unto One's Life, and can be taken untoo a court of Justice, and be compensated for lose. Most cases are heard firstly in a magistrates court before a high court of Justice, some cases may be taken further unto an Imperial Court

However, Likewise can a government take a individual to court, for those whom claim they are not seeking work but are found to be working or accepting pay .

One also has thee right to live without monies and clothes and be appropriately situated within society.

Paid works are works seeking a wage for one's time and services, Seeking paid works disturbs the Equality of the communities benefits, and segregates one another, upon issues of job titles and wage, it also raises the cost of living, As each and every job in the world should only be of Voluntary Service and for the well being of the communities and nation in a whole. Un-fortunately if we do not offer ourselves voluntarily then we will be making thee price of services or merchandise higher due to our own needs therefore raising economy.

People whom follow a Religious beleaf, are able to practice their Human right's if the voluntary job's offered are not suitable unto their Holy commandments or oaths, ie if the works are actually about God (Jah), if the environment is Itill ,Vegetarian, Vegan, kitchens are free from razor sharp kitchen knives etc

A COMMANDMENT , OATH, VOW, is a solemn promise, pledge, or personal or religious commitment that no individual should be threatened in breaking:

No one should be pressured or threatened into signing on at the job centre, if one is not seeking paid work , one is simple not seeking paid work, and is entitled unto a benefit worthy of the price of economy around him or her, The benefit should be enough to support oneself, and not merely survive. However where community programmes and developments are in place, then All monies will be put unto a temple, church or village etc.

Our past History has showed us our benefit amounts that we receive eg 45,00 per week, wood only be sustainable in a community environment, but if our members are dis-interested in community affairs thence our governed amounts wood have to increase due to the price of economy and the working class.

It wood be as putting people whom are concerned with there community at a lower wage than those whom are there for its fall. Thee real question is why money at all?

Philippians 4:11

Not that I speak in respect of want: for I have learned, in whatsoever state I am, *therewith* to be **content**.

FREEDOM PASSES, AND PLANE TRAVEL

"**Freedom of movement, mobility rights** or the **right to travel** is a human rights concept encompassing the right of individuals to travel from place to place within the territory of a country,[1] and to leave the country and return to it. The right includes not only visiting places, but changing the place where the individual resides or work

Each and every individual whom is un-employed and not seeking paid works, due to be-leaf and principles, is entitled untoo a freedom pass. As thee prices of Train and plane fares is directed solely at thee working class,

Again Denial of a freedom pass , May result in, A Court hearing and, one may be compensated.

However People generally will not feel they have this right , if they are not participating in thee Farming, Agricutural Development of there land,

Matthew 5:5
Blessed *are* **the** meek: for **they** shall **inherit the earth**.

LAND AND FARMING AND HOUSING

"For those of you who possess the land and labour but lack capital, We have made credit available at low interest. For those of you who have the necessary capital but do not possess land to work on, We have, in accordance with Our Proclamation which entitled every Ethiopian to ownership of land, establishes offices in every province through which you may be able to acquire land. Those who have neither land nor money will be granted land and a financial loan at low interest. For those of you who possess land , who have financial resources and manpower, We have made experts available to furnish you with the necessary guidance and advice in yor various undertakings." **Haile Selassie the First - November 3, 1959**

The right to adequate housing

Housing is the basis of stability and security for an individual or family. The centre of our social, emotional and sometimes economic lives, a home should be a sanctuary; a place to live in peace, security and dignity.

Increasingly viewed as a commodity, housing is most importantly a human right. Under international law, to be *adequately* housed means having secure tenure – not having to worry about being evicted or having your home or lands taken away. It means living somewhere that is in keeping with your culture, and having access to appropriate services, schools, and employment.

The right to housing is interdependent with a number of other human rights: rights to health, to education, to employment, but also to non-discrimination and equality, to freedom of association or freedom from violence, and ultimately to the right to life.

Freedom of Loud music and House or village neighbourhood party's, is healthily recommended, As equal as quietness

Each and every individual has the right to land, for agricultural purposes, Each and every individual has thee Right to shelter. Each and every individual has thee right to a outdoor River to swim.

THOSE WHOM ARE IN PAID EMPLOYMENT ARE ENTITLED, TO LEAVE THERE WORKS AND BE SHELTERED AND BE IN RECIPT OF BENIFIT AND HAVE THERE MORGAGES PAID FOR, DEPENDING UPON AVAILABILITY AND COST OF REPLACEMENT HOUSING AS A REPLACEMENT HOUSE MAY BE WITHIN A GREATER BUDGET. BUT THE REAL IDEA IS JUST TO ALLOW ONE GOVERNMENT TO PROVIDE FOR ALL,

ALSO THOSE WHOM HAVE BUSINESSES WITHIN THEE BETTERMENT OF SOCIETY, HAVE THEE RIGHT TO BE FUNDED BY THERE GOVERNMENT AND OFFER THERE SERVICES AS CHARITY OR NON TAX. IE A VEGAN RESTRAUNT, A CHILDRENS ACTIVITIE PROGRAMME.

THOSE WHOM WISH TO LIVE IN A OUTDOOR ENVIROMENT, ARE ENTITLED TO DOO SO, AND FUNDING FOR MATERIALS, TENTS , CANOPIES, OR SHEDS MAY BE GRANTED, ALSO ELECTRIC SUPPLIES MAY BE FREELY AWARDED.

HOMELESSNESS, IN NO CIRCUMSTANCES MUST A INDIVIDUAL BE MADE HOMELESS, As thee matter is a simple case of a temporary Hall and sleeping Bags, This matter can be compensated in a high court of Justice and housing officials may be taken from there work positions.

It is usually in cases of theft or violence , these issues may be void and one should generally be in a cell.

PARENTAL RASPONSIBILITIES. Equal Rights Both man and woman once a child is mis-educated upon who is Dad and mum are, is entitled to 3.5 days each with thee child, lest in circumstances a woman is breast feeding then thee child will be left with a woman, with Occasional visitation rights in agree ace with thee couple.
Mainly upon issues of violence will rasponsibilities be void. **As a child is a Gift from thee Almighty and is for all to share and nurture a education within itself, denial of a Man's rights is as a man unknowing.**
Man to has feeding Rights, though this is yet to be seen due to a nations lack of education.

10. And that which is in thee breasts (Of men) is made known? (Holy Qur'an)

Matthew 23:9 And **call no *man*** your **father** upon the earth: for one is your **Father**, which is in heaven.

SCHOOLING.

Right to education

Everybody has the right to an effective education.

Parents also have a right to ensure that their religious and philosophical beliefs are respected during the children's education.

Each and every individual has thee right to refuse schooling for our infants, And shall not feel threatened by thee government or forced, as this can result in a high court hearing and imprisonment or penalty fine. WEE have thee right to practice no schooling and no education whatsoever.Or restrick education unto Bible studies only or other religious Books

NHS MENTAL HEALTH SERVICES

Article 3 No torture, inhuman or degrading treatment

The prohibition on torture and inhuman or degrading treatment or punishment is one of the most important provisions in the Human Rights Act.

It is an absolute right – in no circumstances will it ever be justifiable to torture someone.

- Inhuman acts will amount to torture when used to deliberately cause serious and cruel suffering.

- Treatment will be considered inhuman when it causes intense physical or mental suffering.

- Treatment or punishment will be degrading if it humiliates and debases a person beyond that which is usual from punishment.

Each and every individual has thee right to say no to medication and injections, and if any be forced, then this can result in a High court hearing and result in imprisonment or penalty fine. Those whom are within Spiritual studies have the right to rely solely upon their Bible and river water doctrines for healing.

Many people were forced medication within a NHS research, though many people refused they were threatened with injections, "The case was very simple if i feel for a tablet i can take myself to the pharmacy why was the NHs team acting like they were people's Parents, what is a normal way to act does anybody have an answer since most live un-aware- fully in sin"

Did you Know thee Nhs Teams Duties were only to act upon somebody whom is a Danger to thee community, I.e Somebody who just acts violently, or threatening behaviour, but this can differ in opinion, as nobody should feel threatened unless physical contact has been made As words are mere words and have different meanings unto different individuals. There Other Duties are Down to An individual

whom feels it is necessary to Talk to a Nhs team,
those suffering from depression, loneliness etc. And this practice has been breached on many occasions as they appear to just lock up anybody even when they state they are fine. "Some claim that thee people working in the NHS teams were angry with people in receipt of Disability allowance, and the un-true government members set up a plan to punish them" There medication has been known to enlarge peoples body size, loose sexual appetites, and make people weak and shaky, and in some cases paralyse individuals, There has also been a case of Death after an injection. Just like in the movies, there are good cops and bad cops.

People whom are in receipt of Disability benefit do not have to explain a single thing unto the NHS services or Doctor, as the Benefit team whom reward Benefits are completely another organisation, and each individual has the right to express one's condition through a written letter, and there is a Decision team whom decides.

"The human right to health means that everyone has the right to the highest attainable standard of physical and mental health, which includes access to all medical services, sanitation, adequate food, decent housing, healthy working conditions, and a clean environment."

"Throughout history,
it has been the inaction of those
who could have acted;
the indifference of those
who should have known better;
the silence of the voice of justice
when it mattered most;
that has made it possible
for evil to triumph."

HIM EMPEROR
HAILE SELASSIE I

Born July 23, 1892

UPON ITILL, VEGAN, VEGETARIAN LIFESTYLES. AlSO RELIGION

Each and Every individual has thee right to be housed in A community of such lifestyles.

PROVERBS 23
[19] Hear thou, my son, and be wise, and guide thine heart in the way.[20] Be not among winebibbers; among riotous eaters of flesh:

The Bible is not against the drinking of wine, as wine is a Divine Joy, however the Bible is warning us of broken glass bottles, as many people cannot just simply choose thee safer option of a carton or plastc bottle.

Matthew 9:17

Neither do men put new **wine** into old bottles: else the bottles break, and the **wine** runneth out, and the bottles perish: but they put new **wine** into new bottles, and both are preserved.

UPON CHILDBIRTH

Each and every individual has thee right , to protect thee cord and PLACENTA at child birth, One also has the right to say no to injections. Each have thee right to a naturel river Birth

Creation: **101 Reasons Not to Have Your Baby in a Hospital, Chapter 74 - You don't want your baby's umbilical cord cut "I began to notice that often babies who were very quiet would begin to cry when their cord was cut. They would be very distressed, sometimes crying for more than 30 minutes. The question arose: "Does the baby know about its placenta?" and "Does the cutting of the cord hurt it?" There is now a growing body of evidence to support the view that babies do, indeed, have full awareness at birth (unless they are drugged) and that they do feel Pain. "Shed not the blood of thine own for such is the pathway to destruction and contempt," (Holy piby Iby)**

DISABLED PEOPLES.

Each and every individual has thee right to treat oneself, and has thee Right to A open River to Exercise.

Those whom care for dis-abled peoples are entitled to a voluntary rotor Hospitool, that offer services freely to care for disabled peoples, as no one should have to face this rasponsibility everyday

UPON SEXUALL DESIRES. Equality For One another

Not every individual beleaves in marriage, As many beleave in One Love, So each has thee right to be Housed appropriately unto ones Desires and beleafs, as One whom wishes to be free is not going to be happy if thee world surrounding him disagree. There are many countries that Have Nude (Naked) beaches from North and South America to the Caribbean and Europe.

John 3

[29] He that hath the bride is the bridegroom: but the friend of the bridegroom, which standeth and heareth him, rejoiceth greatly because of the bridegroom's voice: this my joy therefore is fulfilled. [30] He must increase, but I *must* decrease.

In philosophy, **naturalism** is the "idea or belief that only natural (as opposed to supernatural or spiritual) laws and forces operate in the world."[1] Adherents of naturalism (i.e., naturalists) assert that natural laws are the rules that govern the structure and behavior of the natural universe, that the changing universe at every stage is a product of these laws.

WHAT DOES THEE HOLY BIBLE TEACH US UPON LOVE.

1 Corinthians 13 (New life version)
[*Love—the Greatest of All*] I may be able to speak the languages of men and even of angels, but if I do not have love, it will sound like noisy brass. If I have the gift of speaking God's Word and if I understand all secrets, but do not have love, I am nothing. If I know all things and if I have the gift of faith so I can move mountains, but do not have love, I am nothing.

LIFE WOOD BE A PRETTY DULL DESERT WITHOUT LOVE, AND UN-EQUAL IF WOMAN JUST WAIT FOR MAN TO APPROACH THEM, LOVE BRINGS FOURTH DIVINE JOY AND SOUND HEALTH, A GIFT TO BE SHARED BY ALL, THEE MORE THEE MARYHER Wee WILL BE

MAN IS MAN AND WOMAN IS WOMAN, "Wo" unto them a nation that mistakes love for mere words and "Wo" untoo them whom judge upon appearance and Job positions and desrot our nations brotherhoods and sisterhoods, from thou have grace upon thy lips thou shall be satisfied with thee fruit therof.

1 John 3:11 For this is the message that ye heard from the beginning, that we should love one another.

John 13:35 By this shall all men know that ye are my disciples, if ye have love one to another.

PEOPLE ARE SCARED TO KISS ONE I-NOTHER, I AM TALKING ABOUT A REAL PASSIONATE KISS SMOOCHIE NOT JUST A PECK ON THEE CHEEK LOOK AROUND YOU, THEY ARE ALL WORSHIPPING THEE SHOPS AND VANITY

EVERYBODY TALKS BOUT LOVE ,BUT WHOM IS PREPARED TO GIVE LOVE.. ME I AM NOT IN NURSERY, NO DISRASPECT TO THEE LION CUBS BUT YOU KNOW WHAT I AM SAYING ,INSTEAD WEE JUST SAY HI TO ONE ANOTHER MAYBE

Love ye one another, O children of Ethiopia, for by no other way can ye love the Lord your God.(holy piby)

John 15:12 This is my commandment, That ye love one another, as I have loved you.

Romans 13:8 Owe no man any thing, but to love one another: for he that loveth another hath fulfilled the law.

Galatians 5:13 For, brethren, ye have been called unto liberty; only use not liberty for an occasion to the flesh, but by love serve one another.

1 Thessalonians 3:12 And the Lord make you to increase and abound in love one toward another, and toward all men, even as we do toward you:

1 Thessalonians 4:9 But as touching brotherly love ye need not that I write unto you: for ye yourselves are taught of God to love one another.

1 Peter 1:22 Seeing ye have purified your souls in obeying the truth through the Spirit unto unfeigned love of the brethren, see that ye love one another with a pure heart fervently:

1 John 4:7 Beloved, let us love one another: for love is of God; and every one that loveth is born of God, and knoweth God.

1 John 4:11 Beloved, if God so loved us, we ought also to love one another.

1 John 4:12 No man hath seen God at any time. If we love one another, God dwelleth in us, and his love is perfected in us.

2 John 1:5 And now I beseech thee, lady, not as though I wrote a new commandment unto thee, but that which we had from the beginning, that we love one another.

Matthew 22 Authorized (King James) Version (AKJV) 22 And Jesus answered and spake unto them again by parables, and said, 2 The kingdom of heaven is like unto a certain king, which made a marriage for his son, 3 and sent forth his servants to call them that were bidden to the wedding: and they would not come

36 Master, which is the great commandment in the law? 37 Jesus said unto him, Thou shalt love the Lord thy God with all thy heart, and with all thy soul, and with all thy mind. 38 This is the first and great commandment. 39 And the second is like unto it, Thou shalt love thy neighbour as thyself. 40 On these two commandments hang all the law and the prophets.

Thou shalt accept Thy God as thy father and mother as thy pastures accepts thy rain, and ye be thy children therof, for there be none prettier or uglier with acceptance, as each was moulded I-qually of Divine beauty, let no man say this is my child or no woman say this is my son, for thee hour of denial will slowly increase upon them.

Matthew 23:9 And **call no *man*** your **father** upon the earth: for one is your **Father**, which is in heaven.

SMOKING GANJAH MARYWANJAH THEE SACRED HERB

One of thee Greatest cases of thee Human Rights act of thee world even today, thee war too free and legalise her goes on even unto today, For some, herbs is obviously legal "She is a herb, from thee earth, people cut chickens throats and breath in thee smoke in cooking, and they think that is cool, Why doo they fight thee herb"

Thee herb is legal in many states now such as Amsterdam , a proof of how peoples can change thee laws of thee world wee live in. It is all down to movement of our peoples. But it goes to show how hard people must strife together to change thee laws governing them.

Though thee herb can be classed as legal to those whom smoke her, Others of orthodox faith have much debate upon thee cleanliness of hands and whom should distribute her,

Psalm 18:24

Therefore hath the Lord recompensed me according to my righteousness, according to the **cleanness of** my **hands** in his eyesight.

also there are many people whom profit monie too support themselves, and this creates a lesser share for people, Others hope she wood be sealed and distributed nationwide legally as a bag of crisp, And hope each individual wood have there own plantation rights.

In any case thee herb should not be a business to make monie, she is our life and health and study, Only Charity or non tax organisations should distribute her.

This applies also unto Other smoking plants such as Ash thee African stone , Frankincense and myrrh ,also Crack cocaine thee Biblical term White stone, and Heroin though i in no way shape or form am condoning injecting heroin, as this is a sin. It seems like thee real problem with these gifts is thee 3rd world dealers whom are trying to make monies for themselves to support their living and decreasing the amount people should rightfully obtain, but again it is not them alone Solely at fault , just we must educate ourselves upon obtaining benefits and be voluntary workers in the first place. Thee real question wee should ask is how much is Kellogg's corn flakes and who is making monies and why. I shore you will come too thee realisation, all things are free, and miraculously created my only guess that our nation was being punished due to there lack of Grace.

Ephesians 2:8-9

For by **grace** are ye saved through faith; and that not of yourselves: *it is* the gift of God: not of works, lest any man should boast.

UPON ANIMALS, Animal rights

Animals have been denied there rights simply because they refuse to talk English, and there are no accurate translators of thee Animal kingdom's world, as the acient Geez tongues or Hebrew translates, And simple because they have not been to school and been taught to talk English , They must be accepted as a newborn babies or that of a child with special needs, as wee may draw reference unto a parrot whom has learnt to talk.

Some wood say, Animals talk not for obvious Humentarian reason's

Each and every individual has thee right to be housed appropriately, ie, a Dog rechoirs much land and poos (Dung), to farm, Also a Dog has a large appetite and must be fed no less than one feeds themselves, As you will find a Dog is not just in love with Dog food, no a Dog sucks everything. Also A Dog rechoirs much sexual activity, so cannot be alone. This is thee case for much of thee Animal KingDom. Also relations between man and Animal must be treated fairly and respected as no man has thee right to Judge a Animals behaviour without speech.

These are just a few of Our statutory fundamental Human Rights, most people find there meanings within Spiritual Study, as their Origin descends from thee Holy Bible and thee Holy commandments.

Although these are our rights, we are not guaranteed to be heard in a court of Justice, and are sometimes violated. But if one is true to what you be leave , nothing can take your right away, and one will strife hard to work to see that these laws are **manifested.** . "And that generation is *fortunate indeed which learns from other than its own bitter experience."* Selassie I

To develop oneself, one has to develop one's own initiative and perseverance - a man has to strive in order to grow. Let us work out our own programmes in all fields - political, economic, social and military. Man's contributions which live to influence the life and progress of posterity, are the most permanent monuments that can ever be created. We must become increasingly willing to analyze our efforts, to experiment, to admit our failures as we take pride in our successes.Selassie I

It is like saying, if you feel you have not been heard, then look around you, when you can get together with people whom beleave thee same thing, then you shall be much stronger and be able to state your point much more clearly, as you must remember, thee High court judge is just a man in thee streets as your neighbour or friend do not class anybody as above yourself.

And Each and every law is within thee development of your community and nation on a whole, So no one should aim to please themselves.

HOWEVER IF ONE FINDS THEMSELVES ON THERE OWN, THEN NEVER GIVE IN TO THAT WHAT IS RIGHT, UNTOO ONES HAPPINESS AND HEALTH, WHY SHOULD ONE SUFFER UPON ACCOUNT OF ANYONE.

"Of all good things of the world which are accomplished by the wisdom of men and ... by that wisdom, **HEALTH** *is the divine gift which is to be found above all by those who take care to guard it well."* Selassie I 1947 .... Speech *To Navel Cadets*

Although many human right cases have been heard in thee past, they are not always successful, as thee way of life often drowns their views. It is like saying, if one man gets up and states his Human Rights alone, then thee whole world wood be opposing him, as there could be no matter of real importance if only one man is addressing thee court, but this does not make thee one man wrong, this is what is called a Leader. And somebody whom will enlighten others by his own misfortune. As in thee end One can only doo what is right, even if one is alone.

However A True devotee is never alone, High Priest Janoy states" Look upon thee Rivers, these are my people, It is no good talking about Humenity Vegetarian Issues with those whom have no concern in such things."

Though many find they may communicate with thee Creature worlds, It is not so easy to emphasis this in a political vote as of yet, and can be said one is but mind reading one's own thoughts.

Genesis 1:2 And the earth was without form, and void; and darkness *was* upon the face of the deep. And the **Spirit** of God moved upon the face of the waters.

ITHIOPIAN REVISED I-nesis 1:2 And her earth was without form, and void; and darkness *was* upon thee face of thee deep. And thee **Spirit** of Jah moved upon thee face of thee waters.

THEE AGE RESTRICTIONS OF THEE HUMAN RIGHTS ACT, IS DEPENDANT UPON'S ONE KNOWLEDGE OF AGE, AS MANY BELEAVE NOT IN AGE. ONE ALSO HAS THEE RIGHT TO REMOVE AGE FROM ONES DOCUMENTATION.

Isaiah 57:15

For thus saith the high and lofty One that inhabiteth **eternity**, whose name *is* Holy; I dwell in the high and holy *place*, with him also *that is* of a contrite and humble spirit, to revive the spirit of the humble, and to revive the heart of the contrite ones.

THOUGH ONE MAY UNDERSTAND ONES RIGHTS, ONE STILL RECHOIRS EDUCATION TOO FULLY OVERSTAND, AS IT WAS WITH MUCH SPIRITUAL STUDIE IN HOLY BOOKS AND OF HER EARTH AND RIVERS IN ITSELF THAT HAS BROUGHT THIS RELISATION UNTOO YOU,

Human Rights

Colonialism and the policy of racism impose soul searching questions of human rights, weighing equally on the conscience of all men and nations of good-will. History amply shows that the freedom enjoyed by the many becomes fragile when the denial, even to the few, of basic human rights is tolerated.

Our efforts as free men must be to establish new relationships, devoid of any resentment and hostility, restored to our belief and faith in ourselves as individuals, dealing on a basis of equality with other equally free people.

We believe in cooperation and collaborration to promote the cause of international security, the equality of man and the welfare of mankind.

We believe in the peaceful settlement of all disputes without resorting to force.

All well ordered and modern states can only base themselves upon Courts of Justice and Conduct of Laws which are just, correct and geared towards the protection of the rights of individuals. Justice is a product of education.

Man's ingratitude to man is often manifested in willingness to relegate human beings to the scrapheaps of life when they enter the twilight of their careers and younger brains and stronger arms are found to replace them.   Selassie I

And similarly with people who have lived by custom only, without learning at school, without absorbing knowledge by the ear or observing and searching with the eye, it is necessary to accustom them, through educations to abandon habits by which they have for long been living, to make them accept new ways. yet not by hasty or cruel methods but by patience and study. gradually and over a prolonged period.

Selassie I

Self Help

The people themselves must come to realize their own difficulties in the development of their community and try to solve them by collective participation following an order of priority and taking their potentiality into account.

It is well known to you all that recognizing one's problems and striving hard to challenge them is a mark of an attempt at self-sufficiency. Self help in the benefits to be acquired through education, will save the individual from asking someone's assistance. Selassie I

New Way of Life

November 2, 1966

What we seek is a new and a different way of life. We search for a way of life in which all men will be treated as responsible human beings, able to participate fully in the political affairs of their government; a way of life in which ignorance and poverty, if not abolished, are at least the exception and are actively combatted; a way of life in which the blessings and benefits of the modern world can be enjoyed by all without the total sacrifice of all that was good and beneficial in the old Ethiopia. We are from and of the people, and our desires derive from and are theirs.

Can this be achieved from one dusk to the next dawn, by the waving of a magic wand, by slogans or by Imperial declaration? Can this be imposed on our people, or be achieved solely by legislation? We believe not. All that we can do is provide a means for the development of procedures which, if all goes well, will enable an increasing measure and degree of what we seek for our nation to be accomplished. Those who will honestly and objectively view the past history of this nation cannot but be impressed by what has already been realised during their lifetime, as well as be awed by the magnitude of the problems which still remain. Annually, on this day, we renew our vow to labour, without thought of self, for so long as Almighty God shall spare us, in the service of our people and our nation, in seeking the solutions to these problems. We call upon each of you and upon each Ethiopian to do likewise......

Above all, Ethiopia is dedicated to the principle of the equality of all men, irrespective of differences of race, colour or creed.

As we do not practice or permit discrimination within our nation, so we oppose it wherever it is found.

As we guarantee to each the right to worship as he chooses, so we denounce the policy which sets man against man on issues of religion.

As we extend the hand of universal brotherhood to all, without regard to race or colour, so we condemn any social or political order which distinguishes among God's children on this most specious of grounds. Selassie I

The Essence of Power

"The power which you possess is but one side of the coin; the other is responsibility. There is no power or authority without responsibility, and he who accepts the one cannot escape or evade the other. Each one of you and each servant of the Ethiopian nation and people would do well to ponder these words, to take them to his heart, and to guide his conduct in accordance with their teachings. This is the challenge which faces you today. Let your labours here during the coming year demonstrate your capacity to meet it. May Almighty God guide and assist you in your work."

H.I.M. Emperor Haile Selassie I
Closing remarks of speech to
Parliament
November 2, 1966

Money Belongs to No One

The conflict about money is what might be called a "conflict of ownership". But the truth is that money belongs to no one. This idea of possessing money has warped everything. Mon-ey should not be a "possession": like power it is a means of action which is given to you, but you must use it according to... what we can call the "will of the Giver", that is, in an impersonal and enlightened way. If you are a good instru-ment for diffusing and utilising money, then it comes to you, and it comes to you in proportion to your capacity to use it as it is meant to be used. That is the true mechanism.

The true attitude is this: money is a force intended for the work on earth, the worl required to prepare the earth to receive and manifest the divine forces, and it- that is – the power of utilising it – must come into the hands of those who have the clearest, most comprehensive and truest vi-sion.

The Sunlit Path. Words of The Divine mother

Whence one overstands monie and its origin, all that one rechoirs is a pen and paper and time spent upon a letter unto ones benefit provider or government leader, because money really buys nothing much that is truley needed.

MENTAL FORMATION AND PROGRESS

I do not believe at all in limits which cannot be crossed. But I see very clearly people's mental formations and also a sort of laziness in face of the necessary effort. And this laziness and these limits are like a disease. But they are cur-able diseases.... If you are a normal person, well provided you take the trouble and know the method, your capacity for growth is almost unlimited,

There is the idea that everyone belongs to a certain type, that, for example, the pine will never become the oak and the palm never become wheat. This is obvious. But that is some-thing else: it means that the truth of your being, according to your formation, your progress is almost unlimited. It is limited only by your own conviction that it is limited and your ignorance of the true process, otherwise...There is nothing one cannot do, if one knows how to do it.

(The Sunlit Path. Words of The Divine mother)

"OTHERS ARE NOT DOING IT"

What prevents me from opening myself to the (Divine's) influence is the suggestion, "Why hurry, why so soon, since the others are not doing it?"

This is a frightful platitude!

But even if you must be the one and only being in the whole creation who gives himself integrally in all purity to the Divine, and being the only one, being naturally abso-lutely misunderstood by everybody, scoffed at, ridiculed, hated, even if you were that, there is no reason for not doing it. One must be either a tinsel actor or else a fool. Because other's don't do it? But what does it matter whether they do it or not? "Why, the whole world may go the wrong way, it does not concern me. There is only one thing with which I am concerned, to go straight. What others do, how is it my concern? It is their business, not mine."

This is the worst of all slaveries!

(The Sunlit Path. Words of The Divine mother)

But, "Man cannot live by bread alone." Man, after all, is also composed of intellect and soul. ... education in general, and higher education in particular, must aim to provide, beyond the physical, food for the intellect and soul.

H.I.M. Haile Sellassie I Selected Speeches
Sep. 21, 1963

Mentioned 16 times in Scripture, it is a future river that, amazingly, restores physical, mental and emotional health to human beings! It is the proverbial, "fountain of youth!" It also "greatly enriches" her earth. It begins flowing during the menenimum and continues forever.

WHAT DOES HER EARTH REALLY NEED?, DOES NOT LOVE MAKE ALL THINGS BETTER?

Each Must Contribute Let there be no mistake: in modern Ethiopia, each man must contribute. There is no protection from the demand that a man's worth be assessed by his achievements. Education and learning offer no escape from the obligation of toil. Social position and high birth provide no guarantee of soft hands and a life of ease and comfort. High origins are no passport to high position. To those who contribute willingly, to the best of their abilities, who, in sweat and toil, work for the good of the nation with little thought of self, to them will much be given, even to the governing of the land. Nor should anyone today mistakenly believe that only in the cities can he serve his country. The greater need today is among the people, with those who work the soil, who provide the nourishment and sustenance upon which Ethiopia feeds. The University National Service Program has pointed the way. Today's younger generation must maintain their ties with the people who are the bulk and backbone of the nation. The problem of the many must become the problem of the few, for only in this way can the progress we earn be lasting and real and of benefit to all.

My substance shall be for the
Benefit of the whole people. (The protevangelion)

It is *better to till* the land *rather than* to *bicker* on trivial matters. SELASSIE I

On the Bible

We in ethiopia have one of the oldest versions of the bible, but however old the version may be, in whatever language it might be written, the Word remains one and the same. It transcends all boundaries of empires and all conceptions of race. It is eternal.

No doubt you all remember reading in the Acts of the Apostles of how Philip baptised the Ethiopian official. He is the first Ethiopian on record to have followed Christ, and from that day onwards the Word of God has continued to grow in the hearts of Ethiopians. And I might say for myself that from early childhood I was taught to appreciate the Bible and my love for it increases with the passage of time. All through my troubles I have found it a cause of infinite comfort.

"Come unto Me, all ye that labour and are heavy laden, and I will give you rest" who can resist an invitation so full of compassion?

Because of this personal experience in the goodness of the Bible, I was resolved that all my countrymen should also share its great blessing and that by reading the Bible they should find truth for themselves. Therefore, I caused a new translation to be made from our ancient language into the language which the old and the young understood and spoke.

Today man sees all his hopes and aspirations crumbling before him. He is perplexed and knows not whither he is drifting. But he must realise that the Bible is his refuge, and the rallying point for all humanity. In it man will find the solution of his present difficulties and guidance for his future action, and unless he accepts with clear conscience the Bible and its great Message, he cannot hope for salvation. For my part I glory in the Bible.

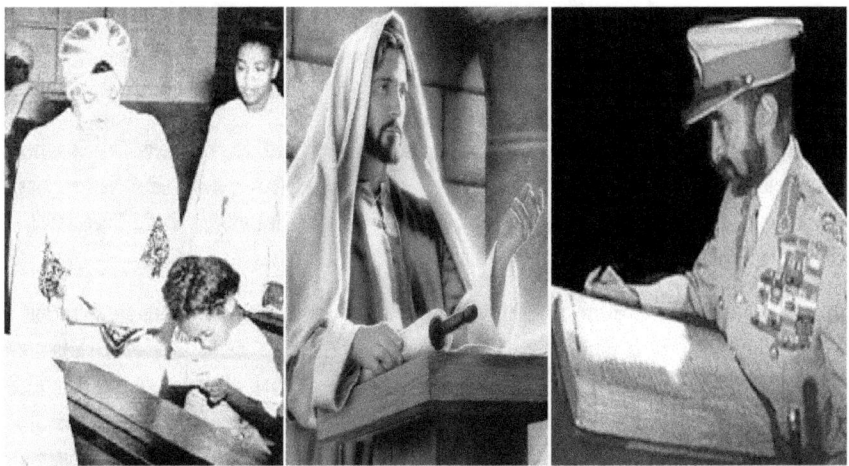

MY BIBLE STUDIES THEE OPEN SCHOOL OF LIFE BRINGING FOURTH NEW LIFE EACH DAY.

Thee Holy Bible is Our Book of life, like any book one chooses to read, you must read page one to thee end, otherwise you wood never overstand thee story. Every individual was born in this world through darkness and sin, and without thee Holy Bible one has no hope to improve ones future, one has no hope of Eternal life and Divine health and immortality. One wood remain a son of man as opposed to a sun of thee Almighty Ones Education wood remain irrelevant by reading ungodly literatures each and every day.

Our Holy Bibles feeds our inner spirits, and it is this spirit that Guides us unto perfection and a new life within thee Divine.

Firstly doo not hold any doubt that your Holy Bible is your Book of Life and Guidance unto a pleasant future and rebirth within thee Divine father and mother, It's worldwide multiplication and number one read Book of all time should assure you, this is a miracle, is there any other Book in thee world that has multiplied worldwide and sits within thee Heart of our nation, that people utter upon every street corner. A inheritance passed on from our ancestors from generation to generation, In fact thee only book passed on from generation to generation.
Secondly Overstand Thee Holy Bible teaches us of eternal life and youth and Creation, and wee must be amongst Creation amongst thee trees, by thee River, listening to thee Ocean to enjoy thee Benefits thee Holy Bible has to offer, It is no good us sitting behind 4 walls or in a church all day, this will steal Thee Holy Bible's Blessings and Light she has to offer. And also rob us of Our Health and true education. It is no use drinking water from thee tap or fruit from the shop each day, then her rivers and trees wood be nothing as to us when judgement falls upon us.
Matthew 6:22 The light of the body is the **eye**: if therefore thine **eye** be single, thy whole body shall be full of light. Matthew 6:23 But if thine **eye** be evil, thy whole body shall be full of darkness. If therefore the light that is in thee be darkness, how great *is* that darkness!

Thirdly remember that God (Jah) created fowls and fish of thee sea and all creatures that creepeth her earth before Us, So have a Open mind unto there teachings and movements, A Dog does not speaketh English to us yet, but yet A Dog has so much to say by one's Actions. A swan thee same.

Fourthly doo not ponder to deep upon verses you doo not overstand, as thee Holy Bible is written in a ancient language, Wee must read every verse as this is exercise for our mind, you may ask, why there is so much talk of negative value, ie, Devil (Dis-mantled village) Evil (Evaporated village) Hell (Handfull of everyday's life's libertys) etc but I will explain.

Thee Holy Bible is as a theatre of today, remember every creature animal human etc is a child of God, So if a chicken is slaughtered to eat, God will say And Cain murdered Abel or shem devoured Ham etc, Wee can not be half hearted upon our feelings of what is good and bad. Also it is God's way of telling us, thee things wee read and sea in life and on Tv, that wee casually condemn but seem to criticize thee Holy Bible, of all thee things wee could criticize eg every other book of thee world that has no mention of God, or every Tv programme, or every restaurant with no grace.

WHY SHOULD WEE RUN FROM THEE ONE BOOK THAT HAS PROVED ITS MIRACLE BEFORE YOU WAS BORN. AND CARRYS ON INCREASING TODAY. Thee Holy Bible is as a puzzle, for us to choose and decide upon thee literature that is of truth and of strength to our nation, eg, some verses mention people eat meat, others show this is a sin, it is for us too follow our inner spirits and find out who our Holy father and mother really are, And this in term wee perfect ourselves by our own Judgements, by taking Time to imagine who God is, If you are a parent you will often question yourself, What wood God doo? How wood he try to change thee world he lives in and make it a better place.

Thee Bible is also said to be magical, So for instance, if our communities our nation were all following thee commandments of being fruitfull vegetarians, then thee negative values in thee Holy Bible wood not exist. It is no use of every page uttering flowers rivers sex and love, if all one can sea is bloody meat, earrings, and concrete , no wee will have to strife to grow, by educating one another with real education

During thee course of your Study, you will have learnt much, and you will feel stronger and stronger, Stronger about Truth, stronger about life ,stronger about faith, stronger about her earth ,stronger about her rivers, stronger about her trees of life ,stronger about her sun shine, and stronger about yourself and purpose in life, and most importantly, Stronger about Our Holy father and mother of Creation.

Psalm 68:4(Authourised King James Version) Sing unto God, sing praises to his name: extol him that rideth upon the heavens by his name **JAH**, and rejoice before him. Matthew 23:9And call **no** *man* **your father** upon the earth: for one is **your Father**, which is in heaven.

HEALTH

"Of all good things of the world which are accomplished by the wisdom of men and which can be realized by that wisdom, HEALTH is the divine gift which is to be found above all by those who take care to guard it well." Selassie I 1947

Thee truth is sex is necessary as often as possible, love helps us smile, helps us survive each day, gives us thee greatest pleasures, meks our bodies healthy and strong, and is vital too thee cycle of life,

No sex meks us , moody, miserable, unhappy wither thee day, weak, wee feel unhappy wither our ippearances, wither one inother,senseless,

Their is no real Health without sex, love for one inother........selassie I

Exercise and yoga practices, keep us sexually motivated, and our innerselfs satisfied. Sometimes wee forget, wee have musles in her legs thighs, in our breast, which wee must exercise, not by lifting weights, which are danjahrous, but by jogging in between thee trees, press ups upon thee pastures, swimming within oceans and rivers, Without swimming , wee are all generally very stiff, We are born from Water and need water too truley know our innerselfs,

Thee Church of ile Selassie I, Inc.

Woe Untoo all thee riches upon her earth for without TS'äga "Grace" I have nothing.

Mine is thee Kingdom of Selassie I

Mine is a Itill Vegetarian Livity

Mine are born from h-earth, Rivers, Trees and Sun, aFor I N I am but thy pastures and ye be thee sheep therof

Mine are born farmers

Mine hold no kitchen swords either nuclear missles or warheads

Mine is Humenity and thee progression therof

Wee Overstand that thee Present Rivers Lakes and Oceans Water Supply can amply statisfy thee needs of Our Nation Worldwide.

This , Together with Other basic facilities that wee have already provided for thee Village of Harer, Wee hope may insure Its Health and Development and accelerate its growth.

Thy womb of Creation, Thy River waters of I-ternal Youth and life within itself, are thee streams of inspiration, pumping new life and reviving our hearts and spirits. Something that money cannot buy.

A Gift of Our Holy Father and Mother TafarI ina Zion.

Life is but a River and ye be thy Trees therof

Menen is a River. It is only later that she came to be identified as thee goddess and Mother of Creation

Exodus 15

²⁴ And the people murmured against Moses, saying, What shall we drink? ²⁵ And he cried unto the Lord; and the Lord shewed him a tree, *which* when he had cast into the waters, the waters were made sweet: there he made for them a statute and an ordinance, and there he proved them, ²⁶ and said, If thou wilt diligently hearken to the voice of the Lord thy God, and wilt do that which is right in his sight, and wilt give ear to his commandments, and keep all his statutes, I will put none of these diseases upon thee, which I have brought upon the Egyptians: for I *am* the Lord that healeth thee.

Revelation 22:2

In the midst of the street of it, and on either side of the river, *was there* the tree of life, which bare twelve *manner of* fruits, *and* yielded her fruit every month: and the leaves of the tree *were* for the **healing** of the nations.

John 10:28

and I give unto them **eternal life**; and they shall never perish, neither shall any *man* pluck them out of my hand.

Genesis 3:22

And the Lord God said, Behold, the man is become as one **of** us, to know good and evil: and now, lest he put forth his hand, and take also **of** the **tree of life**, and eat, and live for ever:

Proverbs 3:18

She *is* a **tree of life** to them that lay hold upon her: and happy *is every one* that retaineth her.

PROTECT OUR CHRISTMAS TREES's

MARY KRISTOS   IGHLYLIJAH

www.ingramcontent.com/pod-product-compliance
Lightning Source LLC
Chambersburg PA
CBHW072256170526
45158CB00003BA/1090